ADVENTURES IN SPACE

YURI GAGARIN
AND THE RACE TO SPACE

Ben Hubbard

heinemann
raintree

To contact Capstone Global Library please call 800-747-4992, or visit our web site
www.capstonepub.com

Edited by Clare Lewis and Abby Colich
Designed by Steve Mead and Justin Hoffman
Original illustrations © Capstone Global Library Ltd. 2015
Illustrated by Justin Hoffman
Picture research by Svetlana Zhurkin
Production by Victoria Fitzgerald
Originated by Capstone Global Library Ltd.
Printed and bound in China by CTPS

19 18 17 16 15
10 9 8 7 6 5 4 3 2 1

Library of Congress Cataloging-in-Publication Data
Hubbard, Ben, 1973- author.
  Yuri Gagarin and the race to space / Ben Hubbard.
    pages cm.—(Adventures in space)
  Includes bibliographical references and index.
  ISBN 978-1-4846-2514-9 (hb)—ISBN 978-1-4846-2519-4 (pb)—ISBN 978-1-4846-2529-3 (ebook) 1. Gagarin, Yuri Alekseyevich, 1934-1968—Juvenile literature. 2. Vostok (Spacecraft)—Juvenile literature. 3. Astronauts—Soviet Union—Biography—Juvenile literature. 4. Manned space flight—History—Juvenile literature. I. Title.
  TL789.85.G3H83 2016
  629.45'0092—dc23   2015000264
  [B]

This book has been officially leveled using the F&P Text Level Gradient™ Levelling System.

Acknowledgments
We would like to thank the following for permission to reproduce photographs:
Alamy: Bill Heinsohn, 15, Joeri De Rocker, 20, RIA Novosti, 17, 27, 28, 35; Dreamstime: Legky, 5; Getty Images: Heritage Images/Fine Art Images, 43, SSPL, cover (bottom), 31; Granger, NYC: ITAR-TASS Photo Agency, 41; NASA, 39; Newscom: akg-images, 7, ITAR-TASS, cover (top), 37, TASS, 13, TASS/Alexei Stuzhin, 4, TASS/Valentin Sobolev, 11 (bottom), Universal Images Group/Sovfoto, 11 (top), 38, Zuma Press/Kommersant, 21, Zuma Press/Kommersant/Ogonyok, 14, Zuma Press/Veronika Lukasova, 29; Shutterstock: Gary Blakeley, 8, Graphic Compressor, 9, joingate, 32, Neirfy, 26, Pavel L Photo and Video, 12, vicspacewalker, 23, 25

We would like to thank Dr. Geza Gyuk for his invaluable help in the preparation of this book.

007333CTPSF15

CONTENTS

All words in bold, **like this**, appear in the glossary on page 45.

YURI GAGARIN: SPACE PIONEER

On April 12, 1961, there was a loud crack in the sky over the village of Smelkovka, in Russia's Saratov region. Around 4.4 miles (7 kilometers) above the village fields, explosive bolts had just blown the escape hatch off the spacecraft *Vostok 1*. Moments later, a parachutist in an orange space suit drifted down toward a farmer's wife and her daughter working in a field. The parachutist was Yuri Gagarin, the first man to travel into space.

"When they saw me in my space suit and the parachute dragging alongside as I walked, they started to back away in fear. I told them, 'Don't be afraid. I am a Soviet like you, who has descended from space and I must find a telephone to call Moscow,'" Yuri Gagarin said.

■ **Crowds of people lined the streets of London, England, to welcome Gagarin in 1961.**

FAME AND FORTUNE

By the time Gagarin reached Moscow, he would be the most famous man in the world. He had beaten his fellow **cosmonauts** to be first into space. The **Soviet Union** had again outdone the United States in the race to space. Everybody wanted to meet Gagarin, shake his hand, and ask about his 108-minute journey into space. He was promoted to colonel, given a **chauffeur**-driven car, and made Hero of the Soviet Union. But despite his great accomplishments, Yuri Gagarin's life would end tragically only seven years later.

A monument marks the spot where Gagarin landed in Russia's Saratov region.

The Soviet Union

The Soviet Union was made up of Russia and 14 countries surrounding it. The **communist** Soviet governments were strict, secretive, and severe in their punishments for disobedient citizens. The United States was the Soviet Union's arch enemy, especially from 1947 to 1991, a period known as the **Cold War**.

CHILD OF WAR

Yuri Alekseyevich Gagarin was born on March 9, 1934, in the village of Klushino, in Russia's Smolensk region. His parents worked on the local farm, which provided food for the state. In the communist Soviet Union, everyone was expected to work together for the common good.

Then, in 1941, **Nazi** Germany declared war on the Soviets and its armies invaded. By 1942, Klushino was caught in the middle of the fighting, and shells rained down on the village. Soon after, German tanks rolled into Klushino and the Nazis took over.

UNDER OCCUPATION

Under the Nazis, Gagarin and his family were forced out of their home and had to live in a mud hut in the yard. Yuri did everything he could to fight back. He smashed glass on the roads to puncture German tires and dropped dirt into the Germans' tank engines.

One day, a Russian fighter plane crashed in the fields near Klushino. Gagarin and his friends ran to help. The pilot handed out chocolate bars to the boys. Gagarin stood transfixed by the plane. "We understood immediately the price that had to be paid for military decorations. We boys all wanted to be brave and handsome pilots," Gagarin said.

V-2 rocket

During World War II, the Nazis developed the V-2 rocket—a terrifying **long-range missile** that traveled at the speed of sound. After the war, **Allied** soldiers captured the Nazi V-2 factories, the rocket plans, and the scientists working on them. Later, scientists in both the United States and the Soviet Union developed the V-2 into a larger rocket that could reach space.

Nazi V-2 rockets like this one were shipped to the United States after World War II so that they would not fall into Soviet hands.

LEARNING TO FLY

At 21 years old, Gagarin trained to become a fighter pilot at Orenburg Pilots' School. He also met and married Valentina Goryacheva. After Gagarin graduated, the young couple was stationed at Nikel Air Base in Murmansk. Nikel was a cold, desolate place only 186 miles (300 kilometers) from the Arctic Circle. Valentina had to raise their first child during long, dark winters in **subzero** temperatures. Gagarin had to fly **MiG** jets through blinding snow and land on slippery black ice. One of his fellow pilots died in a crash within his first month at Nikel.

The jet-powered MiG-15 had swept-back wings, a tail fin, and stabilizers to help it reach the speed of sound.

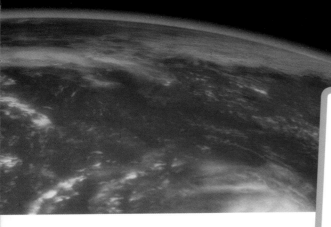

Sputnik 1

On October 4, 1957, the Soviet Union became the first nation to launch a **satellite** into space. *Sputnik 1* was a small metal ball with four radio antennae that sent back information about **Earth's atmosphere**. The "beeps" made by *Sputnik 1* were picked up by radio receivers around the world.

MYSTERY MISSION

In 1959, a mysterious group of recruiters arrived at Nikel Air Base. They carried out interviews with the pilots, but did not say who they were or what they wanted. Gagarin was selected to travel to Moscow to undergo further tests. The pilots had more interviews, were physically examined, and took a math test. During the test, a voice read out incorrect answers over the pilots' headphones as they tried to calculate the correct ones. Finally, Gagarin was asked if he'd like to fly in something more modern than a MiG—a rocket that could fly all the way around Earth.

Focus on:

THE RACE FOR SPACE

The Soviet Union stunned the world when it launched *Sputnik 1* into space. Up until then, nobody realized that the Soviets had such advanced rocket technology. Now, they showed they were capable of firing a long-range missile into the United States. As a result, *Sputnik 1* sparked a "Space Race" between the two nations.

But before the Americans could respond to *Sputnik 1*, the Soviets dealt them another blow by sending the first living creature into space. Less than one month after *Sputnik 1*, *Sputnik 2* was launched with a dog named Laika aboard. It was clear that the Soviets would soon attempt to send a person into space.

GRAPEFRUIT SATELLITE

The United States had to prove it could also send something into space. On December 6, 1957, it attempted to launch a satellite from the Space Center in Florida. But shortly after liftoff, the rocket carrying the satellite exploded. It was a bitter humiliation for the United States. The press called the satellite "Flopnik"— a play on the word "Sputnik."

In January 1958, the United States finally launched its first satellite, *Explorer 1*, into Earth's orbit. Because *Explorer 1* was smaller than *Sputnik 1*, Soviet leader Nikita Khrushchev insultingly called it "a grapefruit."

■ Laika was a stray dog found on the streets of Moscow. She was picked for the *Sputnik 2* mission because she was good at sitting patiently.

Sputnik 2

Laika was a stray dog who was trained to sit in *Sputnik 2*. She was fitted with **sensors** to monitor her heart rate, diapers for her waste, and oxygen tanks for air. It was never intended for Laika to survive the flight, but it later emerged she sadly died from heat exhaustion only six hours after liftoff.

■ Nikita Khrushchev was eager to tell the world that the Soviet Union was winning the Space Race.

COSMONAUT GAGARIN

In 1960, Gagarin and 19 other pilots were short-listed from 2,200 candidates to train as cosmonauts. These trainees would compete to be the first man in space. The group was taken to a secret training center called Star City, hidden deep in the woods north of Moscow. Star City was still being built when they arrived and was only a few basic buildings. Inside these buildings, the cosmonauts faced extreme tests designed to push them to their physical and mental limits.

■ Star City, seen here in 2012, was originally a small, secret base but it grew to the size of a town over time.

SPACE SPEAK

Cosmonaut: A cosmonaut is the Russian name for an astronaut—a person trained to travel into space aboard a spacecraft.

ЦЕНТР ПОДГОТОВКИ КОСМОНАВТОВ имени Ю.А. ГАГАРИНА

STOP

Behind the scenes at Star City, Gherman Titov and Yuri Gagarin (right) had their own mini space race to be the first cosmonaut into space.

LONELY LOCK-UP

The most dreaded tests took place in the "isolation chamber": a sealed room that cosmonauts were locked in for up to 10 days at a time. Doctors on the outside would order the cosmonauts to perform tasks, such as exercise or math problems. This was to observe how humans might cope with being alone in space. In one test, Gagarin was forced to repeatedly write down his name as the doctors reduced the oxygen in the chamber. Eventually, he fainted. After a few days in the isolation chamber, Gagarin began singing a song about the colored wires he could see, to keep from getting bored.

Gherman Titov

Gagarin's greatest rival at Star City was Gherman Titov. When he was 14, Titov had broken his wrist but kept it a secret so it wouldn't spoil his chances of going to flying school. Now, he was a top fighter pilot and determined to become the nation's leading cosmonaut.

TRAINING FOR SPACE

At Star City, Gagarin and the other cosmonauts underwent physical tests that imitated conditions in space. However, no one was sure what space was actually like. The doctors *did* know that a cosmonaut would feel a tremendous weight called a **g-force** when his spacecraft lifted off. They also knew a cosmonaut would have to eject from his spacecraft at the end of his mission. As a result, the cosmonauts practiced parachute jumps from great heights. Gagarin liked the jumps—it was the one place the doctors could not follow him.

■ Parachute training was important for Gagarin (third from the left)—it was how he would land back on Earth.

Human guinea pigs

The doctors at Star City also performed tests on human volunteers. These men were subjected to 40 G's on the centrifuge machine and asked to jump from dangerous heights without protection. Many were badly injured during these experiments.

SPACE SPEAK

G-force: The "G" in "G-force" stands for "gravitational." Humans on Earth constantly experience 1G from the planet's **gravity**. Astronauts usually experience around 3 G's at takeoff. At 9 G's, most people would lose consciousness.

◼ The dreaded centrifuge machine was used for G-force testing on Russian cosmonauts. It is pictured here at the Yuri Gagarin Cosmonaut Training Center at Star City.

STAR CITY SPINNING

Gagarin was used to the g-force created when his jet accelerated fast or turned a sharp corner. However, even he did not enjoy the **centrifuge machine**, which imitated high "G's." The machine worked by spinning cosmonauts around at fast speeds. Gagarin had reached 7 G's in an air force centrifuge machine, but at Star City, the doctors pushed their machine up to 12 G's. Yuri described the experience: "My eyes wouldn't shut, breathing was a great effort, my face muscles were twisted, my heart rate speeded up, and the blood in my veins felt as heavy as **mercury**."

SPACECRAFT

While the cosmonauts trained at Star City, Soviet engineers and designers prepared the spacecraft that would send them into space. The chief designer was Sergei Korolev, a man so important to the Soviet space program that his identity was kept a secret. Korolev had developed the R-7 rocket from the Nazi V-2 rocket and used it to launch *Sputnik 1* and *2* into space. He was then asked to build a spacecraft to carry a man into space. In June 1960, this spacecraft, called *Vostok 1*, was ready to show to the cosmonauts.

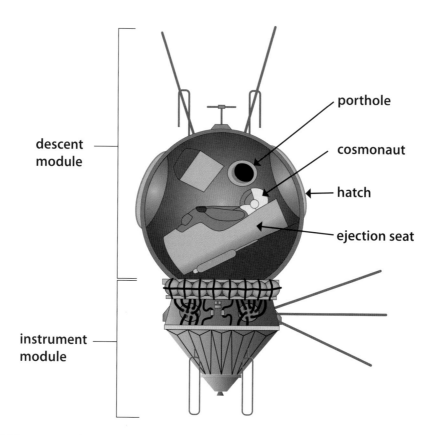

descent module

porthole

cosmonaut

hatch

ejection seat

instrument module

The two main parts of *Vostok 1* were the descent module and the instrument module. They were designed to separate before re-entering Earth's atmosphere.

WINGLESS FLIGHT

Gagarin and the other cosmonauts were amazed by *Vostok 1*—a round flying machine without wings. *Vostok 1* was made up of a **descent** module, where the cosmonaut sat, and an instrument module below it. The whole spacecraft sat above an R-7 rocket. Gagarin was the first to sit in *Vostok 1*, and he quickly noticed the control panel was simpler than in an MiG jet. This was because *Vostok 1* was fully automated and the pilot could only take manual control by entering a secret three-digit code into a keypad. However, the Soviet doctors thought **weightlessness** might drive a man crazy. If there was an emergency on *Vostok 1*, they would only radio the cosmonaut the code if they judged him to be sane.

■ A revolving globe on *Vostok 1's* control panel showed which part of the world it was flying over.

Inside *Vostok*

Vostok 1's **ejection seat** filled most of the padded descent module. In front of the seat, an instrument panel showed the module's temperature, oxygen levels, and its position over Earth. Below the ejection seat was a small **porthole** window, and above it the escape hatch.

Focus on:
SPACE ROCKETS

The *Vostok 1* spacecraft needed the massive power of an R-7 rocket to blast it into space. Like all rockets, the R-7 worked by burning fuel and firing a jet of gas from its **exhaust** nozzles. This shot the rocket upward to reach the required speed of 17,895 miles (28,800 kilometers) per hour. This speed is enough to put the spacecraft into orbit.

The R-7 stored the huge amount of fuel needed in four booster rockets that were strapped to its side. As the boosters burned up their supplies of fuel, they would be released from the R-7 and fall away to Earth.

Shortly after, the shell around *Vostok 1* would fall away to expose the spacecraft. Then, only a core and final rocket would be left to give *Vostok 1* the last push into orbit, before also dropping away.

To stop from being in orbit, *Vostok 1* would have to slow itself down or otherwise stay circling Earth. To slow down, *Vostok 1* would fire its **retro-rockets**. This would allow Earth's gravity to pull the spacecraft out of orbit and back toward Earth's surface.

SPACE SPEAK

Orbit: An orbit is the curved path an object makes in space as it travels around another, bigger object. The smaller object is kept in orbit by the bigger object's gravity. For example, satellites are attracted by Earth's gravity and are kept in orbit around it. The Sun is a much bigger object than Earth and the seven other planets in the **solar system**. This is why Earth and the other planets are attracted by the Sun's gravity and travel in orbit around it.

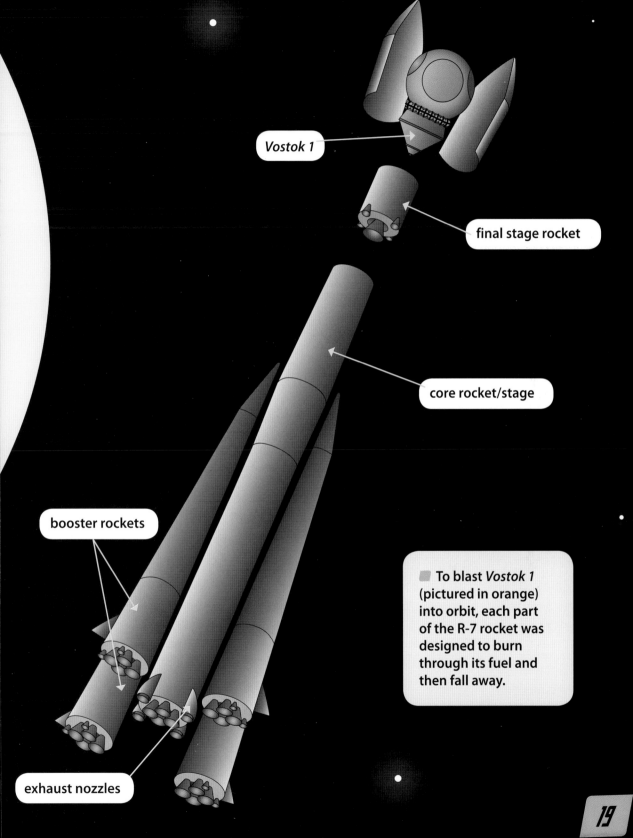

Vostok 1

final stage rocket

core rocket/stage

booster rockets

To blast *Vostok 1* (pictured in orange) into orbit, each part of the R-7 rocket was designed to burn through its fuel and then fall away.

exhaust nozzles

TEST FLIGHTS

In mid-1960, the Soviet Union learned that the United States was preparing to send a man into space. In response, Star City scientists immediately stepped up their own efforts. Over the next 10 months, they launched seven test spacecraft from the secret Soviet Baikonur **Cosmodrome**. Four of the launches, however, ended in failure.

On July 28, 1960, Gagarin and the other cosmonauts were invited to the launch of *Vostok 1K-1*, which had two dogs on board. To the cosmonauts' horror, the spacecraft exploded shortly after liftoff. "We saw how the rocket could fly, more importantly we saw how it blows up," Gherman Titov said. However, on August 19, they sent the dogs Strelka and Belka into space aboard *Sputnik 5*. They orbited Earth 17 times and returned safely, a great success for the Soviets.

SK-1 pressure suit

The SK-1 pressure suit that Gagarin wore was the first space suit ever used in space. A tight, rubberized inner shell helped protect against extreme g-forces. A thin orange outer shell made it highly visible. Its oxygen and ventilation hoses were plugged into *Vostok*'s ejection seat.

■ Gagarin's *Vostok 1* space suit is shown at a museum in Gagarin, the town formerly known as Gzhatsk that was renamed in his honor.

Doctors were worried that Belka (right) had vomited during the dogs' space flight. They wondered if space would also make humans sick.

SPACE SHORT LIST

With only months to go, it was still unclear who would be the first man into space. By early 1961, only two remained in the running: Gherman Titov and Yuri Gagarin. Instead of trying to outdo each other, both cosmonauts were helpful, cooperative, and careful to show team spirit. This, they knew, was the Soviet way.

SPACE Q AND A

Q. How do I become a cosmonaut or astronaut?

A. During the early Space Race, fighter pilots were usually picked to go into space. Today, you need science degrees, flying experience, physical fitness, and lots of determination!

COUNTDOWN BEGINS

Five days before the launch of *Vostok 1*, the announcement was finally made. Yuri Gagarin would be the first man into space. However, the man in charge of cosmonaut training, General Nikolai Kamanin, had struggled with the decision, because it could cost one of the cosmonauts his life. He wrote in his diary: "It's hard to decide which of them should be sent to die, and it's equally hard to decide which of these two decent men should be made famous worldwide."

Years later, Gherman Titov said Gagarin was the right choice, because his big smile and charming manners made him an easy celebrity for the world to love. However, Titov found it hard to hide his disappointment during a dinner a few days after the decision was announced. Here, in front of cameras, the cosmonauts had to pretend they had only just heard the news. Then, Gagarin had to give his "surprised" acceptance speech twice, after the cameras ran out of film the first time. Gagarin said he found the moment difficult. "I was thinking of Gherman… He's an intelligent man and a wonderful friend. He should make the flight, too. I felt rather awkward. Why me? Why not him?"

Weightlessness worries

Although *Vostok 1* now had its commander, the Soviet scientists were still worried about the effects of weightlessness. The feeling of weightlessness in space is caused by the falling of the spacecraft around the Earth as it orbits. To practice in around three seconds of weightlessness, the cosmonauts were dropped down a 28-story elevator shaft onto a big air cushion below.

Gagarin practiced for weightlessness in an elevator shaft. Today, astronauts at Star City prepare for spacewalks by training underwater in swimming pools like this.

FINAL PREPARATIONS

With one day to go before *Vostok 1*'s launch, final preparations began. At 5 a.m., the R-7 rocket with *Vostok 1* at the top was pushed slowly along the railroad tracks at Baikonur Cosmodrome to the launch site. Walking the 2.5 miles (4 kilometers) alongside the spacecraft was its designer, Sergei Korolev. Once the R-7 was lifted to its **vertical** position, Gagarin and Titov practiced their final boarding procedures. As the backup cosmonaut, Titov had to be prepared to replace Gagarin at a moment's notice.

UNEASY SLEEP

Scientists were still observing both cosmonauts as though they were competing to be the first man into space. The night before the launch, Gagarin said he wasn't even slightly nervous. However, the Soviet doctors wanted to be sure. They attached sensors to the mattresses of Gagarin's and Titov's beds to monitor their sleep. Both cosmonauts suspected this. Perhaps a restless night with lots of tossing and turning would cost Gagarin the mission, and give it to Titov. As a result, both cosmonauts spent the night lying as still as possible and neither slept a wink. At 5:30 a.m., Gagarin and Titov were told to go to breakfast. "How did you sleep?" Gagarin was asked. "As you taught us," he replied.

A modern Russian *Soyuz* rocket is transported along the railroad tracks to its launch site at the Baikonur Cosmodrome.

Baikonur Cosmodrome

The Cosmodrome that launched all of the Soviet Union's rockets into space was built in a remote, desert-like area in central Kazakhstan. Building work started on Baikonur Cosmodrome in 1955. Although the real town of Baikonur was nearly 200 miles (320 kilometers) away, it was given this name to keep the site secret from the rest of the world.

APRIL 12, 1961: INTO SPACE

After a cosmonaut's breakfast of brown paste squeezed from a tube, Gagarin and Titov were driven to the launch site. The doctors fixed sensor pads to their bodies and then dressed them in their space suits. Secretly, Titov hoped Gagarin's space suit was damaged, so he could take command of *Vostok 1*. Gagarin, on the other hand, was already experiencing the effects of fame. "The people helping me into my space suit held out pieces of paper; one even held out his work pass, asking for an autograph," Gagarin said.

■ A Vostok rocket is on permanent display at the All-Russia Exhibition Center in Moscow.

The launch site

Vostok 1 and its rocket were transported horizontally to the launchpad and then raised skyward. Massive steel support gantries then held the 101-foot- (30.8-meter-) high rocket in place. These would fall away upon liftoff. Flames from the rocket would fire downward into a pit beneath it.

■ Once strapped into *Vostok 1*, Gagarin had an hour to wait before liftoff.

GOODBYE GAGARIN

The two cosmonauts were driven by bus to the launchpad. "The closer we got to the launching, the larger the rocket grew… It looked like a giant beacon, and the first ray of the rising sun shone on its pointed peak," Gagarin said.

When the bus stopped, Gagarin tried to say goodbye to Titov with kisses on his cheeks, but in their space suits, they could only bang helmets together. Then, Gagarin got off the bus and Titov stayed behind. Before entering the elevator on the launch **gantry**, Gagarin turned and waved to the state officials and cameras. Three minutes later, he was standing at the top of the gantry beside *Vostok 1*.

PREPARE FOR LIFTOFF

At 7 a.m. on April 12, 1961, engineers helped Yuri Gagarin wriggle into *Vostok 1* and plugged the life support hoses from his space suit into the ejection seat. Now, Yuri was part of the spacecraft that would fly him on autopilot around the world and back to Earth. By 8 a.m., the technicians had sealed the hatch. Gagarin could only take control of *Vostok 1* by using the manual override keypad—but he was not officially allowed to have the three-digit code. However, before the engineers screwed on *Vostok 1*'s outer hatch, one tapped on Gagarin's helmet and whispered the numbers to him. "I know," Gagarin replied. "Kamanin's already told me." Years later, Gagarin revealed Sergei Korolev had also broken the rules and given him the code.

Vostok 1 blasts off from the Baikonur Cosmodrome.

Gagarin's liftoff description

"I heard a whistle and an ever-growing din, and felt how the gigantic rocket trembled all over, and slowly, very slowly, began to tear itself off the launching pad."

■ This desk-sized guidance computer helped to send Gagarin into space.

"LET'S GO!"

As Gagarin waited patiently inside *Vostok 1* during the final checks, he requested that some music be played over the radio. He was asked how he was feeling. "Fine, like they taught me," he replied.

According to the sensors on Gagarin's body, he was calm and had a normal heart rate. With all systems checked, the music stopped and Korolev's voice came over the radio: "Yuri, the 15-minute mark." Gagarin put on his gloves and closed his helmet's visor as the mighty R-7 engines rumbled into life. Then, at 9:07 a.m., Gagarin shouted out, "Let's go!" as *Vostok 1* blasted off.

108 MINUTES

Two minutes into the flight, Gagarin was thrown forward in his seat as the four booster rockets burned through their fuel and fell away. Then, a tremendous g-force pulled at Gagarin's face muscles as the central core rocket took over. "Continuing the flight, g-load increasing. All is well," Gagarin reported on his radio back to Earth.

After three minutes, the shell covering *Vostok 1* at the front of the R-7 rocket fell away. Now that the spacecraft was exposed, Gagarin caught his first glimpse through the porthole of dark blue below him. After five minutes, the core rocket dropped away and the final rocket fired into life. After ten minutes, the final rocket also dropped away, and Gagarin could feel the vibrations stop. Then, *Vostok 1* was in orbit 200 miles (321 kilometers) above Earth.

After the final rocket fell away, all that was left was the instrument module and descent modules that took Gagarin around Earth.

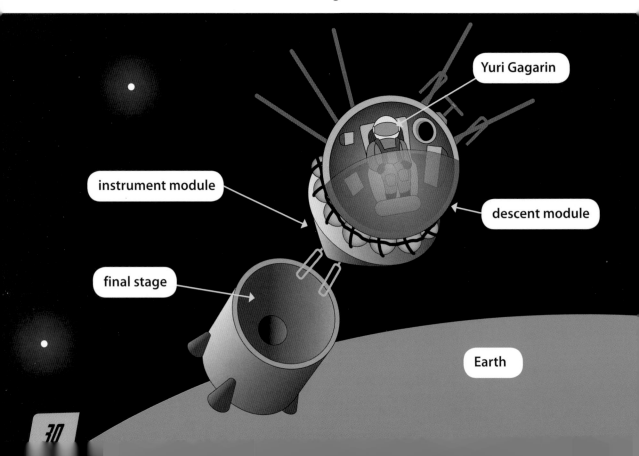

Yuri Gagarin

instrument module

descent module

final stage

Earth

Breaking news

The Soviet news agency TASS had been sent three envelopes before the launch of *Vostok 1*, each reporting a different outcome about the flight. Now the envelope reporting the successful launch of the first man into space was opened and proudly broadcast on Radio Moscow.

■ A model of *Vostok 1* with its final rocket attached is displayed above a picture of Earth.

SPEEDING THROUGH SPACE

As Gagarin passed eastward over Siberia, the control panel showed that *Vostok 1* was traveling at 17,895 miles (28,800 kilometers) per hour. "Weightlessness has begun. It's not at all unpleasant, and I'm feeling fine," Gagarin reported. *Vostok 1*'s onboard camera recorded Gagarin playing with a weightless pencil and a globule of weightless water. Below him, Gagarin could see the curve of Earth's horizon and the thin layer of its atmosphere.

MODULE MALFUNCTION

During the flight of *Vostok 1*, Gagarin sent constant updates to Soviet **tracking stations** on Earth. "The flight continues well," Gagarin reported. "The machine is functioning normally. Reception excellent. Am carrying out observations of the Earth. Visibility good. I can see the clouds. I can see everything. It's beautiful!"

Thirty minutes after liftoff, *Vostok 1* crossed over the Pacific Ocean. On this side of the world, the Sun was setting and night was about to begin. As darkness fell, Gagarin was able to view the stars through *Vostok 1's* porthole for the first time.

▨ ***Vostok 1's* flight path is shown from its liftoff in Kazakhstan (1) to its touchdown in Saratov (7).**

1. Launch
2. In orbit
3. *Vostok 1* passes into darkness above the Pacific Ocean
4. *Vostok 1* emerges into daylight above the Atlantic Ocean
5. Retro-rocket fire for re-entry
6. *Vostok 1* re-enters Earth's atmosphere
7. Gagarin lands back on Earth's surface

Vostok around the world

It was important that the Soviets kept in regular contact with *Vostok 1*, but the spacecraft traveled over countries where the Soviet Union did not have tracking stations. To fix this problem, the Soviets built mobile tracking stations on seven ships and sent them out around the world's seas and oceans.

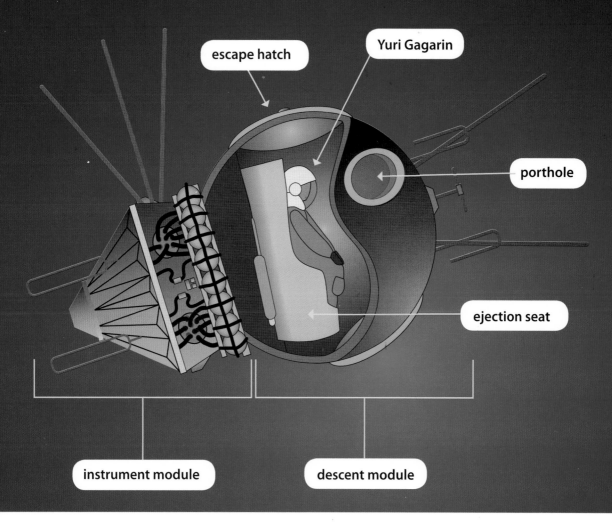

escape hatch

Yuri Gagarin

porthole

ejection seat

instrument module

descent module

■ Once he had plugged his life support systems into the ejection seat, Gagarin was part of *Vostok 1*. To leave the spacecraft, he would have to eject with the seat through the escape hatch.

NIGHT INTO DAY

After 64 minutes, *Vostok 1* crossed over the Atlantic Ocean and back into daylight. As the spacecraft traveled over Africa, it automatically started the preparations for re-entry. At around 10:25 a.m. Moscow time, *Vostok 1*'s retro-rockets fired to rapidly slow the spacecraft down so Earth's gravity would pull it out of orbit. At the same time, an explosive charge was supposed to separate the instrument module from the descent module. But this didn't work—several wires still held the two modules together. Suddenly, both modules began to go into a spin as *Vostok 1* fell back toward Earth.

FALLING TO EARTH

As *Vostok 1* plunged toward Earth, it spun dangerously out of control. The temperature quickly rose inside the spacecraft as it re-entered Earth's atmosphere. To make matters worse, the spinning created an unbearable g-force, which nearly made Gagarin pass out. But luck was on Gagarin's side. The intense heat of re-entry burned through the stray wires connecting the two modules and the instrument module broke free.

World record

Although Gagarin parachuted to Earth separately from *Vostok 1*, this was kept a secret for years afterward. To claim the world **aviation** record for sending a manned spacecraft into space, both the man and the spacecraft had to land together. Gagarin and the Soviet Union pretended this had been the case with the *Vostok 1* landing.

As the instrument module finally fell away, Gagarin and the descent module parachuted separately to the surface.

The descent module came to rest in a field.

PARACHUTE PLUMMET

Gagarin, however, was still not safe from danger. At 4.4 miles (7 kilometers) above the ground, *Vostok 1*'s hatch blew away with a great crack. This was supposed to happen, but the ejection seat was also meant to fly out at the same time. Instead, Gagarin and his ejection seat were still inside the module. As *Vostok 1* plummeted toward Earth, Gagarin had to decide when to eject himself. With the g-force again becoming intense, Gagarin ejected at 3.8 miles (6 kilometers) above the surface. This time, the automatic systems worked. The ejection seat's parachute opened, and 108 minutes after liftoff, Gagarin drifted safely down to the ground.

SPACE Q AND A

Q. Did U.S. astronauts also have to eject from their spacecraft?

A. U.S. astronauts landed on Earth inside their spacecraft and did not eject from them. However, astronaut Neil Armstrong once had to eject from a practice lunar module called "The Flying Bedstead."

MOST FAMOUS MAN IN THE WORLD

Only minutes after Yuri Gagarin had landed in the fields near Smelovka village, military helicopters appeared as if from nowhere. Gagarin was the new great hero of the Soviet Union and was quickly whisked away to Moscow. As news broke about *Vostok 1*, Gagarin became the most famous man in the world. Up until then, the mission had been so secretive that even Gagarin's family members were kept in the dark until they heard the news on the radio.

In Moscow, Gagarin met Soviet leader Nikita Khrushchev, who awarded him the nation's highest honor: Hero of the Soviet Union. A massive crowd turned out in Moscow's Red Square to celebrate Gagarin's achievement.

Vostok remains

Children from Smelovka quickly found the smoldering *Vostok 1* descent module, which had landed 1.2 miles (2 kilometers) away from Gagarin. They helped themselves to tubes of space food containing chocolate paste and mashed potatoes. Before long, the Soviet military arrived to retrieve the module and its contents.

SOVIET SMILE

The celebrations did not end in the Soviet Union. The whole world wanted to meet the first man in space and hear his story. Gagarin traveled around the globe to meet kings, queens, heads of state, and huge crowds everywhere. Gagarin charmed everyone with his smile and willingness to answer endless questions on space and weightlessness. Secretly, though, Gagarin found all the attention exhausting. "There were tens of thousands of scientists, specialists, and workers who participated in preparing for this flight. I feel awkward because I am being made out to be some sort of super-ideal person," he said.

■ Gagarin said he could see "the streets of Moscow were flooded with people" gathering to welcome him home.

SPACE RACE CONTINUED

The success of *Vostok 1* was a bitter blow for the United States, as the Soviets once again showed they were ahead in the Space Race. To make matters worse, the United States had been about to send astronaut Alan Shepard into space at the time of *Vostok 1*, but the mission had been delayed. Finally, on May 5, Shepard spent 15 minutes in space aboard the Mercury spacecraft *Freedom 7*. Unlike the top-secret *Vostok 1*, the Mercury mission was broadcast to millions of television viewers across the globe. In response, the Soviet Union launched new Vostok missions, including *Vostok 2*, piloted by Gherman Titov. The United States launched more Mercury missions in reply. Then, President John F. Kennedy amazed everyone when he announced the United States would put a man on the Moon by the end of the 1960s.

■ Being an expert parachutist helped Valentina Tereshkova become the first woman into space.

First woman in space

Valentina Tereshkova, from Russia, became the first woman in space when she traveled aboard *Vostok 6* on June 16, 1963. She spent 71 hours in space and orbited Earth 48 times. The flight was another victory for the Soviet Union, but a Russian woman would not visit space again for another 19 years.

■ The *Freedom 7* mission proved that the United States could also send humans into space, although only into sub-orbit.

COSMONAUT COLONEL

After a while, Gagarin returned to his duties at Star City. He was put in charge of the female cosmonaut training program and later promoted to colonel. However, he was also expected to attend many official occasions in Moscow and overseas. Although he was given a chauffeur-driven car and his own room at a luxury Moscow hotel, his new celebrity status took its toll on Gagarin.

A FALLEN STAR

In 1963, Gagarin was appointed deputy director of the Cosmonaut Training Center at Star City. This was a promotion, but it was also a way of keeping Gagarin out of trouble. Gagarin had injured himself after drinking too much and jumping off a hotel balcony. The incident had embarrassed Gagarin and the Soviet Union. Gagarin's days as a cosmonaut were now numbered. In 1967, Vladimir Komarov was killed when his re-entry parachute did not open during the *Soyuz 1* mission. The Soviet Union could not risk losing its national hero, Yuri Gagarin, so he was **grounded**.

FINAL FLIGHT

The Soviet government didn't even want Gagarin to fly jets, but he insisted. On the morning of March 27, 1968, Gagarin and an instructor took off in a two-seater MiG from an air base near Star City. However, at 10:31 a.m., traffic control lost contact with Gagarin. Something was wrong. At 4:30 p.m., the wreckage of Gagarin's MiG was found in the woods around 60 miles (96 kilometers) northeast of Moscow. There were no survivors. Details of the accident remained top secret for decades. It later emerged Gagarin's MiG had become caught in the **backwash** of a supersonic Su-15 jet, which had flown too close. It then crashed into the ground at top speed. Gagarin was dead at 34 years old.

Gagarin's zip code

After *Vostok 1*, Gagarin received so many letters that he was given his own zip code: Moscow 705. Often, Soviet citizens wrote asking Gagarin to use his influence to help them, such as to find them better housing. Gagarin helped whenever he could.

There was a massive outpouring of grief in the Soviet Union as its citizens mourned the loss of their national hero, Gagarin.

GAGARIN'S MESSAGE

Although Yuri Gagarin's life ended in tragedy, his historic spaceflight marked a milestone for humankind. Twenty years before the launch of *Vostok 1*, people could only dream of visiting space. At that time, the V-2 rocket was being developed to end human life (as a bomb) rather than help people to explore space. Strange, then, that it was V-2 technology that led to the R-7 rocket that launched *Vostok 1*.

It also began the Space Race between the United States and the Soviet Union, as each tried to outdo the other. Sometimes this meant corners were cut and people died, because speed was considered more important than safety. However, it also meant that they made quick scientific progress. Many of the technologies developed for space during this time went on to improve everyday life for people on Earth.

Space technology on Earth

Space industry technology has been used in many everyday objects that we take for granted. These range from food wrappers created from the reflective film on spacecraft to **micro**-parts developed for space and used on Earth to make artificial limbs.

PEACEFUL PLANET

Yuri Gagarin's spaceflight united the world in admiration, as people everywhere celebrated this historic human accomplishment. With his big smile, Yuri Gagarin brought people together wherever he went, regardless of what they believed in. For the only man who had seen the planet from space, Gagarin's message was always one of peace on Earth. "Circling the Earth in my orbital spaceship I marveled at the beauty of our planet. People of the world, let us safeguard and enhance this beauty—not destroy it!"

Gagarin won the hearts of the world with his smile, space stories, and messages of goodwill.

TIMELINE

March 9, 1934	Yuri Gagarin is born in the village of Klushino, in Russia
1944	Nazi Germany fires the first V-2 rockets against targets in France and England
1955	Work begins on the Baikonur Cosmodrome, the Soviet space program's launch site
1957	Yuri Gagarin graduates from Orenburg Pilots' School and marries Valentina Goryacheva. The Soviet Union launches the *Sputnik 1* satellite into orbit around Earth.
January 31, 1958	The United States launches its *Explorer 1* satellite into Earth's orbit
1960	Yuri Gagarin is selected alongside 19 others to become a cosmonaut as part of the Soviet space program
May 1960–March 1961	The Soviet Union attempts to launch eleven spacecraft into space, but only seven are successful
April 7, 1961	Yuri Gagarin is selected to be the first man sent into space as commander of *Vostok 1*
April 12, 1961	*Vostok 1* is launched into space. It spends 108 minutes in Earth's orbit and then returns to Earth.
May 5, 1961	U.S. astronaut Alan Shepard is launched into sub-orbit for 15 minutes aboard Mercury spacecraft *Freedom 7*
May 25, 1961	U.S. President John F. Kennedy announces that the United States will land a man on the Moon by the end of the decade
1963	Valentina Tereshkova becomes the first woman in space aboard *Vostok 6*. Yuri Gagarin is appointed deputy director of the Cosmonaut Training Center at Star City.
1967	*Soyuz 1* commander Vladimir Komarov is killed during re-entry to Earth when his parachute fails. Yuri Gagarin is grounded from further spaceflight.
March 27, 1968	Yuri Gagarin is killed when his MiG jet crashes

GLOSSARY

Allied countries, such as Great Britain, France, the United States, the Soviet Union, Canada, and others, who joined together as the Allies, to fight the opposition in World War II

aviation flying or operating aircraft

backwash backward current created by something moving quickly through the air

centrifuge machine spinning machine that simulates high gravitational loads on a cosmonaut or astronaut

chauffeur person hired to drive another person around in a car

Cold War state of hostility that existed between the Soviet Union and the United States and other western countries from 1947 to 1991

communist country (or person) that follows the political system of communism, which states that all property and goods are owned by the community and everyone works according to their own ability and needs

Cosmodrome Soviet launching site for rockets and spacecraft

cosmonaut astronaut belonging to the Russian, or former Soviet Union, space program

descent falling or moving downward

Earth's atmosphere protective layer of air and other gases that surrounds the planet, allowing living things to survive

ejection seat device that lets a pilot eject from his or her moving aircraft or spacecraft in an emergency; also called an ejector seat

exhaust waste gases expelled as a result of an engine burning fuel

gantry high framework designed to support a rocket before it launches

g-force short for "gravity-force," a force of gravity, high loads of which are felt during rapid acceleration

gravity pulling force that attracts objects to one another and prevents weightlessness

grounded ordered away from flying aircraft, spacecraft, or any other flying vehicle

long-range missile missile (rocket) that can be aimed and fired at a target thousands of miles away, causing serious destruction of the target

mercury heavy, silvery-white metal that is liquid at normal temperatures

micro very small

MiG nickname for a Mikoyan-Gurevich fighter aircraft, used by the former Soviet Union

Nazi member of the National Socialist German Workers' Party, which ruled over Germany during World War II

porthole small, round window found on a ship or spacecraft

retro-rocket small rocket on a spacecraft to slow it down for descent onto the Moon or re-entry into Earth's atmosphere

rocket cylindrical object that is driven upward by burning fuel and expelling the gases to push it into flight

satellite object that orbits a star, planet, or asteroid. Satellites can be natural, such as the Moon, or human-made, such as *Sputnik 1*.

sensor device that detects and records heat, sound, or movement. Sensor pads can be used in medicine to measure a person's heartbeat.

solar system Sun, with the eight planets, plus asteroids and other bodies, that orbit around it

Soviet Union (full name, the Union of Soviet Socialist Republics, or USSR), union of Russia and 14 surrounding states, dissolved in 1991

subzero below freezing; extremely cold

tracking station place that monitors the movement of spacecraft, ships, or aircraft using radar

vertical standing straight up rather than horizontally across

weightlessness not feeling the effects of gravity

FIND OUT MORE

BOOKS

Astronaut Travel Guides (series). Chicago: Raintree, 2013.

Brake, Mark. *How to Be a Space Explorer.* Oakland, CA.: Lonely Planet, 2014.

Morris, Neil. *What Does Space Exploration Do for Us?* (Earth, Space, and Beyond). Chicago: Raintree, 2012.

Parker, Steve. *Space Exploration* (How It Works). Broomall, PA.: Mason Crest, 2011.

DVDS

Stephen Hawking's Universe (2010)
The world-famous cosmologist explores the mysteries of the universe, including the Big Bang, the origins of the universe, and the search for extraterrestrial life.

The Universe (2009)
This is a documentary exploring what we know about the outer reaches of the universe.

Wonders of the Solar System (2010)
This series investigates our solar system.

PLACES TO VISIT

Kennedy Space Center, Merritt Island, Florida
www.kennedyspacecenter.com
The Kennedy Space Center features exhibits about space technology and observation decks that look down on the rocket launch sites and the launch control center.

The Museum of Science and Industry, Chicago, Illinois
www.msichicago.org
This museum features a collection dedicated to the history of space exploration.

Smithsonian National Air and Space Museum, Washington, D.C.
airandspace.si.edu
The Smithsonian has an extensive collection of interactive exhibits and objects related to the history of space exploration.

WEB SITES

Facthound offers a safe, fun way to find Internet sites related to this book. All of the sites on Facthound have been researched by our staff.

Here's all you do:
Visit www.facthound.com
Type in this code: 9781484625149

HOW CAN I FIND OUT MORE?

Look in more detail at the lives of the other figures involved in the Soviet space program. Sergei Korolev, for example, was a fascinating character whose existence was kept a state secret and the extent of his contributions not made public until after his death.

Compare the roles of today's cosmonauts and astronauts with those during the Space Race. Today, former Cold War enemies the United States and Russia cooperate in space, but some things are still kept separate.

INDEX